The
Pocket
of
Poems

JULIANA ADA-NNENNA NWAKAMMA

authorHOUSE®

AuthorHouse™
1663 Liberty Drive
Bloomington, IN 47403
www.authorhouse.com
Phone: 833-262-8899

Published by AuthorHouse 04/19/2021

ISBN: 978-1-6655-2343-1 (sc)
ISBN: 978-1-6655-2342-4 (e)

The Pocket of Poems:

My Yesterday and Tomorrow

By

Lolo Mrs. Juliana Nwakamma

To my husband and my children;

my parents, brother, and sisters;

my aunts, Agatha, Dorothy, Leticia,

and the late Fidelia;

my uncles; my brother-in-law, Ebere Anyanwu;

my cousins, nieces, and nephews;

my friends and coworkers;

and mostly to my late father, Pa

Augustine Ndubueze Nwuzor

ACKNOWLEDGMENTS

I want to start by thanking the Almighty God that has made it possible for me to accomplish this goal. I would not had been able to be whom I am today without the efforts and sole support of my parents, with whose help I was able to pass through the four walls of a university. I am grateful to my one and only senior brother, Vincent Nwuzor, who geared me up academically and helped me out of challenges growing up. My special thanks goes to my lovely mother, Ezinne Veronica Nwuzor, who strived under rain and sun to guide me through adolescence by understanding the difficulties of life and the paths of growing up and becoming a woman.

My children—Deraa, Oge, Amy, Johnny, and Kenny— are the best gifts to have happened in my life, because they understand every step that I make or take and support me when am falling down. They are my heroes.

My sisters, Chioma and Okwu, are the best sisters in the world; they are very supportive whenever I reach out to them.

My enormous love and gratitude goes to my husband, Chief Benedict Nkemdi Nwakamma, my better half and my confidant. I cannot ask for more than having you beside me.

My special thanks to a brother, friend, and age-mate, Mr. Mathias Iwu, for his brotherly support. My big thanks to the Iwu family, the Korie family, Mr. and Mrs. Christian and Georgy Egwim, and the Obodo family for their various forms of support. I say a very big thanks to all who have ever been there for me. Initially, it looked like an insurmountable challenge, but I am glad I broke through, and to God be thy glory.

Lolo Mrs Juliana Ada-Nnenna Nwakamma

PREFACE

One very quiet evening, after coming back from school under the hot sun, I found myself very far in deep thought. Suddenly I picked up my pen and started to write. I was in the Nigerian equivalent of middle school when I felt this touch, around thirteen to fourteen years old. I was very good in my literature class, and my literature teacher picked up interest in my writing. He started guiding me as I wrote a play, and as I gradually grew in my writing skills, and my interest in writing became very high. My teacher would proofread my writing and make any necessary corrections, until he felt sick and weakened in the cold hands of death, may his soul rest in perfect peace.

This was the end of my writing at the time, because I did not have anyone to direct, proofread, or make corrections. I got diverted into sports, which became the path to my leaving Nigeria in search of greener pastures in the United States. When I got to the US, with all the challenges and hustling on the street to survive, my dream for writing went unrecognized until the summer of 2006. I enrolled in a Baltimore community college to continue my education and pursue nursing as one of the surviving professions for immigrants. Literature was one of my favorite classes then, and my coursework continued to progress.

There came a day when the lecturer instructed everyone in the class to bring out a sheet of paper and pen. We all followed her instruction while waiting for the next step. She said to everyone in the class, "I want you all to write a poem. Think of something and write."

Of course, no one was expecting that, nor was I prepared as well. I held the pen in my hands, lost in thought, figuring out what to write. Suddenly a title came to my mind, like a whispering voice: "The Outcast." I was confused at first because of the title and how I could possibly link the title to what I did not even know how to write. How to make a match? But before I could imagine what to write, I was already done.

I stood up and submitted my ten lines of poetry, very simple but deep in literal meaning. Little did I know that this same poem would give me the award of the best literature student in that class. On the last day of class, my lecturer presented to me a gift, wrapped and covered up, as the best literature student. I had more enthusiasm than patience as I hurried up to see what was inside the gift. Behold, it was my poem titled "The Outcast." I closed my eyes in hot tears of joy, amazed and shocked. My lecturer designed my poem within a picture frame, and at the bottom of the frame portrait she wrote: *Poem written by Juliana McCullough. Good job and continue writing.*

This was how my dream of writing poems started, and since 2006 I have been actively pursuing the goal of becoming a poet, despite the challenges of being a student and a mother, rearing children from infancy through young adulthood, not to mention working and being a wife.

Husbands are the most difficult children to manage because you have to satisfy their needs for the family to function well and be healthy.

A little about myself. I am Lolo Mrs Juliana Ada-Nnenna Nwakamma, née Nwuzor, the daughter of the late Pa Augustine Ndubueze Nwuzor and Ezinne Veronica Nwuzor. I am from the eastern part of Nigeria, in Obowu Local Government Area in Imo State, mainly from Avutu Dikenta, and married to Chief Benedict Nkemdi Nwakamma from Umuasonye in Umuariam, still in Obowu. I was born at the Mbaise general health center in Imo State. I spent my youth in Lagos State, which is known as one of the busiest cities in Nigeria. Here I attended elementary school, high school, and university, at which point was ready to face tomorrow. My coming to the US was no accident but rather a result of my talent and love for sport. I started with volleyball and soccer, in which I featured at a national level, and in 1997 represented Nigeria under Judo Foundation Sponsorship in judo competition held at Chicago.

I attended Baltimore community college in 2006 to obtain courses for nursing electives. I was admitted in 2007 to the LPN-BSN cohort program at Mountain State University, West Virginia. I graduated in 2009 and at the time of this writing am a correctional registered nurse working as a nurse supervisor in the COVID unit. For the love I have for education to further my career, I joined the mental health industry and I am presently a student of the Psychiatric nurse practitioner at Maryville University and later transferred to Walden University still holding the large heart of love for the literature world.

I am delighted to have accomplished my heart's desire of becoming a poet. I am a mother of three lovely daughters and two stepsons. I am very glad to have the five of them as a family, and I love them so dearly. My story would not be complete without mentioning my husband, my soulmate and my friend—a vibrant, funny character, caring, with a talented wisdom for proverbs and everything I wish to love in a man. I was able to achieve all this because I have wonderful parents who stood beside me and supported me at the mention of anything, and finally, because I have God as my pillar, the beginner and the finisher. I am very grateful that he did not leave me on my way but followed me all through this journey.

TO GOD BE THY GLORY!

The Contents

THE OUTCAST

All in the middle forest

I hear the cry of a naked woman

Help! Help! ... the voice disappears in the wind

She was given away for rituals

An innocent blood was shared

The Ancestors whispers in anger

Justice must prevail

The goddess of *Ikuku* demands for war

The blood must be returned

The Outcast must return ...

BY JULIANA ADA-NNENNA NWAKAMMA

OGBANJE, THE PASSIONATE CHILD

Ogbanje my lost child

Your soul was buried in the deep forest

The forest of the forbidden

Your presence kept tormenting our peace

We did not understand the beating of your drum

Freedom was misunderstood for violence

Long sleepless nights of anguish

A child like you is no more in our midst

We lost a gifted child without knowing

The language and the footsteps were blindly not seen

The voice of the great Oracle" sang once again

Free Ogbanje! Free OGBANJE!

Free Ogbanje, the faithful child.

BY JULIANA ADA-NNENNA NWAKAMMA

THE SORROWS OF A LONG JOURNEY

Down the hill on a lost land

A pathway that became a true destination to a wonderland

A land full of injustice and humiliations

The cry of the innocent is a usual ceremony

No comfort for human race

The indigenes are the kings on the street

No place to hide, if you don't eat on the king's table

A tradition from the old generations

You cannot read the handprints on the wall

While sitting on the fence all day

It takes a very long journey

A journey that has just begun

BY JULIANA ADA-NNENNA NWAKAMMA

DEATH

Death, just as your name sounds

You are very heartless and unpredictable

You miserably knock without warning

Takes without minding what is left

Inside you, is full of sorrows and agony

You dry up the moonlight face of the young child

You like the heavy waves of the ocean that twinkle

the sea

Your rewards are just very few

You force to be everyone's friend

Even when you are not needed

You promised never to rest

Dancing your tail around the neighborhood

Claiming fragile weak souls

When will you get tired of stealing

For the end days are few seconds apart

When the death shall rise again!

BY JULIANA ADA-NNENNA NWAKAMMA

THE AGONY

The Auricles are consumed with laughter

Watching the foolishness of your stained hands in the

splashes of the innocent blood

The anger of Amadiohia the great king of the Ancestors!

Swings like the moving ocean with its shadows of doom

Leaving invisible signs of quietness

The Auricles lifted their angry eyes in the hot sun of the

EKE market day

Beating the drum of the great Masquerade dance

The revenge of an innocent blood

But the wicked heart of man was deaf to hear the agony

from their voices and to see the pain from their dry

tears

You have failed to see and hear the footsteps of death

swinging to your door

Reminding you of the Ancestors' fight and the end to

your path.

BY JULIANA ADA-NNENNA NWAKAMMA

THE UNREALISTIC DREAM

Fantasy the world of empty memories

Taste sweeties but ugliest as felt

Reality the fairest journey, when shadows lead the way

The brave is quick finding home

"Home" the realistic step to adventure

So, journals got lost seeking home, and some

became instrument of history

Only few minded souls found the way home to whom

they really were

From the beginning before the race began.

BY JULIANA ADA-NNENNA NWAKAMMA

THE FORBIDDEN CHILD

Why come knocking when you were only a shadow

Why show your sweet tender smiles

When it was only a path

Why those gentle crying

Reminding me of my nightmares

Why the sweet dreams

Knowing it wasn't going to last

Days becomes night and sleep runs off my eyes

Like the early morning flowers

The thoughts of your emptiness put ages on my weak

bones

I forbid this child... My love that I can never have

BY JULIANA ADA-NNENNA NWAKAMMA

THE SADNESS OF YESTERDAY

Sadness as the word inspires

Eats up the fleshes of my heart

Leaving behind fragile brittle life

Man walks without strength and naked

Weakness engulfs the beautiful smiling face that is

now the symbol of wrinkles

Drawing the quickness of aging closer

The face with the look of an early morning dove

Is stint deep with the scanty hot tears

Opening the challenges of tomorrow

Tomorrow with its unknown features could be the

end of the haggard life

Hanging on life by the string of voices

Arising a new identify as the wind blows by.

BY JULIANA ADA-NNENNA NWAKAMMA

THE CAGE OF YESTERDAY

Fortune as it reads in our heart

Took a lot of minds to their early graves

Families denies oneself for the pursue of life

Lives were crutched and abandoned

Children cried out for help as empty life's lies cold to
their faces

The less privileged dances to the drum

The drum without a heart

The beaters sat on the fence with their faces widens
up with songs and smiles

The little caged child of yesterday, leads the heritage
of tomorrow

What a decade of captives had we lost searching for
fortune

BY JULIANA ADA-NNENNA NWAKAMMA

THE LOST SOUL

Far from the desert bush, the aguish began

Faces were missed in the survival race

The tears of the little minor's flow like the angry wind

of *"Umunmiri*

The great River of the Ancestors Guideship!

Where souls are consumed and stolen away from

their roots

Leaving their branches spread all out in the air

A home of comfort now script of painful memories

Siblings fight among selves as souls were turned

against each other

Home becomes a far misery to reach with its memories

dancing around the heart

The voices yield out in the middle of the rain pour

As it awakes our spirit that the journey just began

And our souls shall find home again and again.......

BY JULIANA ADA-NNENNA NWAKAMMA

THE UGLY CREATURE

You ugly creature with the face of a vulture

You took the beautiful appetite of the lonely child

Leaving him hungry and nauseous

The thought of your face burns like the pain from my

wicked stepmother

At day, you smile like a friend and at night your cut is

like the sharp Leopards bite

Oh! You man of an ugly creature

You have no shame and feelings

You betch on any tree as you fly

You hurt without minding the hurter

Tomorrow is not in your hands as you arrogantly feels

Dropping the gold as a symbol of your emptiness.

BY JULIANA ADA-NNENNA NWAKAMMA

THE MOVING SEA

As the sea swing its winds, the breeze flews around
its island

The air carries its scent beyond the eyes of men

The breeze warns against danger

It's quick like the consumption of death, leaving no
options for decision making

Chances is like leaves blowing off from the tree, so also
is the life of men

Once lost, can't be the same again

The weight of life becomes meaningless

Days runs endlessly as the eyes fights the strength to
close

Showing the heritage of a man as the sea flows by

BY JULIANA ADA-NNENNA NWAKAMMA

THE FORGIVENESS

As the early morning enfolds itself, becomes the worries

of my unclean hands

How it all started a misery adventure

Sitting back to those flashbacks of bitter memories

and victimizations

Aguish engulfs my sinking mind that bleeds with regrets

I see the hands stained with blood

In the dark of all darkness, a deep voice was heard

"You killed that child"

Your hands are soaked in his blood

The blood of a motherland stranger

Whom you made a visitor in his own land

The land flamed up with lighting of anger

Forbidding to take more souls

Forgiveness! The Ancestor bleed for sacrifice to rest

the sleeping troubled soul

BY JULIANA ADA-NNENNA NWAKAMMA

FAREWELL

Farewell the young hero of the Ancient Eastern Coast

The home of your bones holding the stigma of your
umbilical cord

The warrior of your days, their dreams and hope

Painfully, the journey in a wonderland had stopped
you abruptly

You are known for your kindness and your gentle
smile of passion

A smile that reminds me of the helpless infant

You are a victim of injustices and sorrow

Even when you were helpless to fight

Yelling out for the unreachable help, as the steps
became far and more faraway

You have touched our hearts in special ways

Everyone with their own memories

Your soul was gentle like your innocent face

You took every step so peaceful

But the worries and wickedness of life has snatched
you away from us

Alloy! One thing is very certain ...

Your soul is resting somewhere in peace.

A place that knowns no evil, no pain and no suffering

We can still close our eyes and feel your presence,

because you were a good young man

Just as we close our eyes in tears, our hearts are full

of hope that we shall see you again

Bye, my friend and your friends say Farewell!

Until we meet, again where justice is real

Your family will miss you more

Your humble soul will give them the invisible comfort

that money or we cannot buy

Farewell with our hearts heavy and eyes full of tears

before your sudden transition

You left a hole deep in our hearts and your footsteps

will not cleanse from our memories

Rest in the most perfect peace with all our love ...

BY JULIANA ADA-NNENNA NWAKAMMA

THE WISE FOOL

My heart bleeds for the bitter sadness

My trust betrayed the real self in me

The voices of whisperers kept me miserable at the

dark nights of the silent wind

A clear loud voice reckoned to me from a distance

You are the portrait of the wise fool, who puts

everyone else first before self

Who indulges for equality, love and unity until the

very end of reality

When the mirror becomes very visible and the

handprints very legible

Watching the footsteps slowly fades away with the

long lonely night

The pain engulfs and humiliates my existence

The human in me was long gone, leaving traces of

how fooled I had been

With thoughts and flashes of an old scrabbled wound

BY JULIANA ADA-NNENNA NWAKAMMA

A HERO IN OUR MIST

You were the people's musical voice

In the days of your child-Adulthood,

Reality and honesty were your delicacy

The sound from behind was ignored

The voice sang and fades slowly in the darkness

The hero in you was deep sleeping

Seeing reality as anger engulfs our dignities

Empty shadows rattling around us

Your name is a hero just like the sun sets shinning

blames in our weak hearts

The thoughts of you was like yesterday becoming today

Reminding us the memories of a hero lost and gone

BY JULIANA ADA-NNENNA NWAKAMMA

GONE TOO SOON

Why him and why now

Why so sudden and why in the dark of all darkness

When none of us could hear you calling out for help

You struggled and gently closes your eyes in pain

Sadness, my little hero, friend and a brother

I'm going to miss our company driving home which

now a thing of the past

The day seems so empty and long without your gentle

voice calling me "Big Uncle"

When challenges engulf your mind

Goodbye, my friend even though is very hard to accept

the truth

Goodbye my little one as you depart to your new home

where peace is assured forever

A place with better Uncles, Aunties, Friends and the

best Father waiting for you

Rest in perfect peace with my heart full of love for

the time well spent with you

Go well to your new perfect home!

BY JULIANA ADA-NNENNA NWAKAMMA

THE PAIN OF A MOTHER

My eyes are covered with tears reminding me of my
mystery yesterdays
When my days has no difference between days,
evening and nights
The echoes of the gunshots left my weak eyes sleepless
Chasing me deeper into the busy forest
Running in between the trees with my precious baby
as sleep revolves over him
My mind was filled with emptiness with no destination
The only life inspiration was my little angel who lies on
my back peacefully to sleep
I watch day becomes evening to night with no food and
no one to talk to
The sound of the gunshot ran through my back and I
thought my only hope was gone
I ran and ran until where I could hear no more sound
just to feel my jewel
The look of his quietness kept me thinking he was gone

Until my hot tears dropped hard on his face blinking his eyes wide open with a rough smile

I called him my gift from God

It was just me and him in that forest just as the years grew so fast, I watched him became a man

I feel lonely when his voice is far from me

I remember those days of running inside the bush with gunshots leading the way

My hot tears are flowing back again

"Why me my Son" ...

How quick did you forget my comfort back that shielded the days of fragileness and helplessness

Today is your time to shield me, but your sight and voice seem too faraway

Would you ever return? Before my weak eyes close finally to eternity

The pain of a mother can never be replaced with gifts and riches of the world

Make hence before the chicken hacks its egg.

BY JULIANA ADA-NNENNA NWAKAMMA

MY LOST LOVE

The anguish from my heart burns like the hot boiling vapor

The painful tears gushing down my eyes weakens my beautiful eyeballs

The thoughts and flashes back of yesterday is a bundle of nightmares

My love flew away without a trace

Leaving empty broken pieces of love scattered all over my memories

The dreams reflect the sound of warnings where caution retraces my walk through the rough paths

My dreams are hanging off the sling

How can I carry on with the empty promises?

Knowing well that fantasy has taken over my world of lost hopes

As I find myself dancing on the fence with a broken heart visualizing the unknown tomorrow

BY JULIANA ADA-NNENNA NWAKAMMA

THE HATRED

My name is hatred

I have no conscience, feelings nor pity

I am not remorseful of my actions

Sadness and heartbreaks are my targets

Every soul I touch feels my vacuum

I come with no warmings

I am not appreciative of anything positive

I love to see tears run down those eagle eyes

I drive joy to see disappointments

Sometimes I wonder who I am

The painful flash back of memories, manipulations,

torture, humiliations, hatred and rejections

Kept singing in my ears I was a victim

I wish I would never remember those days

When tomorrow seems faraway...

I thought I would never stand again

You are who you are determined to be

Certainty may change your personality, but your

image will always remain your real picture

Just time and only time can heal your inner pains

And then you will become very strong to face the

hard tomorrow

BY JULIANA ADA-NNENNA NWAKAMMA

THE END

The swinging of the peaceful sea, reminds me of your easy exit

You sound like you were there, but all I see was your untouchable shadow

Your invisible absence feels the empty vacuum, which no one can see

You blinded my imaginations with fantasies

You painted your symbols at every step I take while playing your charming games

I was consumed in my world of dilemma

Your steps appears very clear with cautions

You look very dearly before all eyes

I am the only one with the inner eyes who knows your traits and sees your emptiness

How bitter to know that you were never there from the beginning

The end opened my eyes to tears of reality

Your invisibility widens up as you exit out of my life

I am weak and hurting with no choice

Farewell to your new destination and I wished never to see you again.

BY JULIANA ADA-NNENNA NWAKAMMA

THE VICTIM

A journey we both started

Left in the middle of nowhere speechless and sad

Empty and lost!

What kept you so long from coming home

My eyes are weak and running out of tears

My heart beats with fears and rejected

My hope is lost and gone

My memories of yesterday left my old bone brittle

My head is so weak to think

Because of my fears of facing tomorrow alone and
lonely

I am going to miss your smell my dearest love

Because I just realized I was a victim

BY JULIANA ADA-NNENNA NWAKAMMA

THE SECRET OF A SMILE

The beautiful smile of you

Colors the world like a rainbow from the sky

Full of joy and fun

Your presence is amazing to the faces of all around you

Your gentle smile puts more life to the wrinkled faces

Your portraits are invisible

Everyday seems like a lullaby

Your smile mimic the gentle touch of a newborn

Your personality are not easy to come by

You are one in a million

A really good fellow indeed

A God-fearing seed growing glamously

Your swing makes age a number in your skin

You deserve all the beauties that life showers around you

Because you are just a good fellow

A good fellow in indeed.

BY JULIANA ADA-NNENNA NWAKAMMA

LIFE IN AN ENCLOSURE

Manliness as it feels

Lost hopes as usual

Memories overriding realities

Mixed thoughts with a symbiotic empty brainstorming

Yesterday gone and tomorrow loses its values

Devised generation with scattered milestones

Crying and agony now the soft music of the day

The invisible dreams diminish the anguished situations

You cannot interpret the feeling

While holding the hands of the victim

Injustice, humiliation, and victimization the eloquent
features

Your voice weakly fades into the empty path

Leaving the eyes invisibly close

As it awaits for justice to prevail...

BY JULIANA ADA-NNENNA NWAKAMMA

THE BROKEN FEELINGS

My heart cries for peace

Bitter and ugly, my memories leaves hot tear on my

face like tribal marks

Looking at the mirror, flashes painful happiness with

lies

Dealing with my instinct, my biggest circumstances

My body makes the steps, angrily fails to grieve the

moment

My heart bleeds for help with no bearings

The road seems far with unrealistic directions

A little hope hanging on the sling was all that was left

Hearing the voice with the echoes of pain from the

invisible distance

Facing tomorrow becomes a tragedy

As I grieve drunk in my own tears...

BY JULIANA ADA-NNENNA NWAKAMMA

ALL BUT A NIGHTMARE

Thinking and dreaming, a love bundle

Very peaceful lost in rattling painful thoughts

Smiling in the hidden with some unimaginative

uncertainties

Laughing aloud to fill up my dreams

Dreaming without a trace as I lie in between the

hands of confusion, sadness and reality

I wonder If 'am dreaming or walking?

Dinning with a stranger, my realized dilemma

My soul feels hurt as I dace helplessly

Trying to film the realness of today from the past

Watching the day slowly crawls into night was heedful

Without a touch of "WHO I AM" the most

unremorseful feelings

My inner self-sounds like a defeater

As my eyes now captures the evilness from the

distance

My brain snapped visualizing the hidden

nightmare from the sweet beginning

Just a reminder of wasted painful Nightmares!

BY JULIANA ADA-NNENNA NWAKAMMA

ETERNITY YOUR HOME GRAND-PA

Farewell Papa! Farewell Papa!

It is sad to imagine your vacuum

It beaks the seed in me to watch you depart

My breath sinks deep inside me

When I remember your meaningful proverbs

Tears dances off my eye balls

You are known and called the "Great Dike" of your days

In your days, you were a warrior as was called "The

Folktale of Proverbs"

Looking deep in the dark; I can still see your gentle

smiling face

So tender like a dove and calm like the sleeping child

Today, I say farewell with joy to the most peaceful

paradise

Because I know, your soul is resting in peace with

comfort and no pain

Go well! Beloved Papa to a new home of eternity.

BY JULIANA ADA-NNENNA NWAKAMMA

HARD TO SAY GOODBYE

How do you choose to start with your colors of many
characters?

What line would the reading starts from?

How could you look her on the face to begin?

What lies do you have to say this time?

Your manipulations, heartlessness, deceitfulness,
hands stained with empty barrels, and sorrows

Your sins fished you out and you could not hide
anymore.

The truth has broken your shell

Your nakedness now like the cloud revolving round
the sky

You belch from one lie to another like the monkey
enjoying the tree hopping

What episode of your music is left unplowed?

Your time, a mirror before your eyes

You broke my heart leaving yours spreading to no
destinations

You left me tearful, sorrowful and crying

Just take the goodbye as you disappears in the air

Growing up and picking up the pieces will not be with you this time again

Goodbye and goodbye for good with your smell seizing out of me.

BY JULIANA ADA-NNENNA NWAKAMMA

THE NEGATIVE AFFECTION

When love breezes up from the wrong setting

It becomes a basket of sorrows, liars and bosom

gestures

A symbolism of disturbances that leads the way to bed

and awakes before your eyes

Drops you empty like the world sitting on you

When pretense leads the root, fantasies becomes your

companion

Hearing words in parables, drew more confusing touches

"Who is fooling who" the unanswered question!

Failing myself and resisting the emotions my challenges

As I found myself painfully loose into his warm arms

Enjoying the miseries fading slowing to fill the vacuum

for another agony....

BY JULIANA ADA-NNENNA NWAKAMMA

MY RESISTANCE

I feel the breeze echoing down one pleasant cool
evening
The sunshine was all gone in the closet
Giving way for the beautiful admires
This glamour picture reminds me of a love still alive in
my heart
His face kept smiling at me in my dreams making it
hard to look away
This strange face leaves me restless and makes me
longing for dreams
It gives me chills of a forgotten sorrows, pains and
pleasures
In my thoughts, I wished to run to a hidden place
From the freedom of this innocent, romantic,
tempting handsome, and seducing charming face
Facing the challenge was my miserable option
Until this quiet evening, we both ran into the
vibrating feelings

Feelings of how we needed, cherished, and belongs
to each other
We followed our minds that opens up the angels in
our darkness
He is my dreams that appears clearly on the street
His inviting physique sweeps my foot and left me
lifeless
Like the morning storm from the harmattan breeze
His gentleness and soft smile seized the breath in me
His touch stopped the flow of blood through my veins
His curdling hands paving its way to my supporting
weak shoulders puts my eyes to sleep
I could not resist him; just his touch puts me in the
loving motion
Just the thoughts of him. I see the stars falling down
from the sky beyond me
He is my Resistance; my life stops without him my germ!

BY JULIANA ADA-NNENNA NWAKAMMA

A GIFT PASSION

Today is a gift

A package filled with time, beauty and love

Inside you are millions of miles waiting to be shared

Today is a gift clamoring with sunshine

A smile from a stranger with tears of goodbye and

touches of love

Today is a gift freely given with no exempts

Only if we could cherish and uses it before its eloquences

The steps once missed, can never be fixed again

Love is a privilege and a gift

A gift that is so passionate and homely in your heart.

BY JULIANA ADA-NNENNA NWAKAMMA

THE HEART OF A MAN

Man as you are called, where is your conscience?

How are you quick to forget the scripts?

Your heart reminds me the taste of a bitter-leave

looking ugly in the rejected bush

The thinking of a man is as poisonous like a snake's bite

The acts you do, so dangerous like the lion's dent

Your laughter a frightened step of a ghost

Your gift so welcoming like the sound of death

Your heart a whole and too envious of success

Your smile like the killing mixture of the native herbs

Your weakness becomes real as the heart cries pouring

out the truthfulness of a pure wounded heart.

BY JULIANA ADA-NNENNA NWAKAMMA

MY HARD WORK

Only the fools calls themselves brave

A hero is unknown by his good work

A leader is born with engraved personalities

A personality that can be reckoned in a few

You are known for the traits in you

Sometimes the wind blew to challenge the gem in you

You are like a studded diamond

A precious stone in the mist of others

The thought of you is an observation of value

Most times your uniqueness makes you a jewel

Today marks the beginning of a generous character

Continue your kind gestures as your beautiful heart

speaks for you

When the risen esteem of our hope becomes present.

BY JULIANA ADA-NNENNA NWAKAMMA

THE MOTHERLESS PAIN

The pain I feel, I cannot explain

The flash of the dark memories runs down my thoughts

Days of misery, shading of blood and misfortunes

Anger took over the deliberation of reasoning

My cries invisible before all eyes, but very visible in my
eyes leaving a scattered marks

I am soaked in thoughts, regrets, blames and emptiness

Why can't I be like others with laughter?

My surrounding echoes the invisible crying of a baby

My visions are torn apart, searching deeply and
emotionally for motherhood.

My baby, my world that I threw away in the swim of life

Days as it goes leaves a reflection of mirror before
my eyes

Looking for a comforter makes it even harder

My negligence cost me my jewel

I blame the pursuit for life

Only if I could change it, but beholds too late is the
reality

My jewel was gone with the passage of life

Leaving me lonely with a confused mind

The End hurts "the cry of a motherless"

Your pain, maybe consequences of what you did in

the hidden

That nobody saw, but today you cannot run away

from your shadow!

I was a victim, save yourself a victim.

BY JULIANA ADA-NNENNA NWAKAMMA

THE LAMP OF OUR JOURNEY

Who are you? The Legend is my name

The "Giant of all Giants"

The Iroko tree of all Women

The hero of the helpless

The hope of the victims

The breaker of poverty

The light in the desert

The fortress of their movements

The beginner of their journeys

The journey that ended up with you

You gave them an exposure that money cannot buy

A personality like you, is like legend standing by itself

All challenges are simplified once you speak

Paving the pathways that became a reality today

Those helpless victims of yesterday are back from their

long journeys

Wondering in lost coast, seeking for future

A future that starting by your dreams and hidden

visions

You led them into the world for a greener pasture

Without a trace of coming back to you

A child never forgets home, despite the decades

The blood will always seek for Heritage

The heritage that will be missing without you

Sitting on that wheel-chair going through the call of
aging

You are as beautiful as yesterday

A woman with a heart of Gold

You are not two in our Era

The beginning and the lamp of our journeys

We love you so dearly MUMMY...

The journey has just begun. Keep still and enjoy

This is what your fruits sowed back to you

WE ALL LOVE YOU...

BY JULIANA ADA-NNENNA NWAKAMMA.

A MESSAGE TO MY DAD

Papa, if only I could change the hand of the clock. I will move it back to your date of birth. I had wish you could stay more time with us. Behold your time was up and there was nothing any of us could do even when we tried to stop the hand of death. Sitting and visualizing the beautiful moments of parenthood spent with you filled the vacuum. How you had thought us well to be contented with whatever we have and wait for God's appointed time. You brought the real persons in us by teaching us how to practice kindness, love, compassion and prayerful. These in one put together makes you our hero, the best father and a unique personality. Keep staying well Papa and may your kind gentle soul rest in ever lasting peace. Until we see to depart no more. Bye for now Papa. With love from all our hearts; your wife and children. We will always remember your soul. Go well and continue to go well.